First *Journeys*

By Pamela Rushby

Series Literacy Consultant
Dr Ros Fisher

PEARSON
Longman

Pearson Education Limited
Edinburgh Gate
Harlow
Essex CM20 2JE
England

www.longman.co.uk

ISBN 0 582 84139 9

Colour reproduction by Colourscan, Singapore
Printed and bound in China by Leo Paper Products Ltd.

The Publisher's policy is to use paper manufactured from sustainable forests.

10 9 8 7 6 5 4 3

DK

The following people from **DK** have
contributed to the development of this product:

Art Director Rachael Foster

Martin Wilson **Managing Art Editor**	**Managing Editor** Marie Greenwood
Janice English **Design**	**Editorial** Marian Broderick
Brenda Clynch **Picture Research**	**Production** Gordana Simakovic
Richard Czapnik, Andy Smith **Cover Design**	**DTP** David McDonald

Consultant Philip Wilkinson

Dorling Kindersley would like to thank: Fred English for orginal illustration; Simon Mumford for cartography; Polly Appleton for additional design; Julie Ferris, Penny Smith and Selina Wood for editorial help. Rose Horridge, Gemma Woodward and Hayley Smith in the DK Picture Library. Johnny Pau for additional cover design work.

Picture Credits: AKG London: 8tl, 9tl, 12cr2, 18t. The Art Archive: Bibliotheque Nationale Paris 6. B.C. Archives: 15b. Corbis: 22tl, 23br; Bettmann 18bl, 24tl, 24-25; John Madere 11br. Canadian Pacific Railway: 14t, 15t. DK Images: Beaulieu Motor Museum 17b, 18br; National Maritime Museum 7cr; National Railway Museum York/Science Museum 13; Pitt Rivers Museum 4tr. Mary Evans Picture Library: 16; Leadenhall Press 4b. Getty Images: Adam Smith 5b. The Kon-tiki Museum, Oslo, Norway: 11tr. NASA: HSFC 29cr, 29b; JSC 29tr, 31tl, 31tr; KSC 30; MSFC 28l. National Air and Space Museum, Smithsonian Institution: 1tr, 23tr; Smithsonian Institution 22b. National Motor Museum, Birdwood, Australia: 19b. Newspix Archive/Nationwide News: 23cl. Novosti (London): 26b, 27t. Pa Photos: EPA 3, 10tl, 10bl. Reuters: 5t. Science & Society Picture Library: National Railway Museum 12bl. Science Photo Library: 1b, 12cr, 17t; Novosti 27b, 28b. Roger Viollet: 7tr. Special Collections and Archives, Wright State University: 20cr, cr2, 20-21b, 21tr. Jacket: Corbis: Bettmann front t. DK Images: Beaulieu Motor Museum back; National Railway Museum, York front bl.

All other images: DK Dorling Kindersley © 2004. For further information see www.dkimages.com
Dorling Kindersley Ltd., 80 Strand, London WC2R ORL

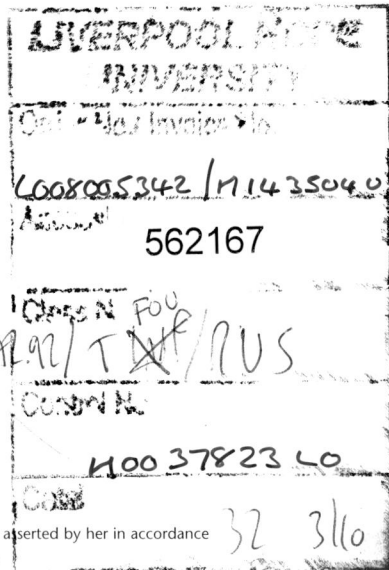

Contents

First Journeys

Every day people board aeroplanes, high-speed trains or jump in a car to go on a journey. However, travel was not always so easy.

The first travellers moved from place to place on foot. Later, people rode on horses, camels and donkeys. About 5,000 years ago people started using wheeled vehicles to transport themselves and their goods. About this time the ancient Egyptians were using boats.

Compasses helped the first Chinese explorers to navigate long journeys.

Steam power drove the earliest engines.

Travelling by plane is now a common event.

Travel did not improve much over the thousands of years that followed. Then in the 1800s travel started to change. Steam trains and steamships dramatically changed travel on land and at sea. After this point increasingly powerful engines were developed.

Throughout history, people have tried to find better ways to get from place to place. This has led to the invention of boats, ships, trains and cars. From here people have gone on to invent aeroplanes and spacecrafts, pushing the boundaries of speed and distance further and further.

Owning a car makes it easier for people to travel.

Boats and Ships

No one knows who invented the first boat. Some early cultures used boats made of animal skins stretched over wooden frames. Many other early cultures used dugouts, which were boats made of hollowed-out logs. The first sailing vessels probably originated in Egypt 5,000 years ago. For thousands of years, people travelled by boats and ships over seas, lakes and rivers. Then, around 2,500 years ago, the world's first major canal was built in China.

The Grand Canal of China

China's Grand Canal was built to carry goods from the Chang Jiang (or Yangtze River) in the south to cities in the north. It was started just over 2,000 years ago and was extended many times. In 605 the Sui emperor Yangdi came to the throne of China.

Yangdi decided to extend the Grand Canal to unite northern and southern China. In 610, the emperor celebrated the opening of the Grand Canal with a parade of thousands of boats. In a land where rivers flow from west to east, a canal that flowed from north to south had a huge impact on the movement of people and goods.

The Grand Canal, which is more than 1,600 kilometres long, remains the world's longest canal.

Admiral Zheng He's Voyages

Zheng He (jung huh) was born in 1371 to poor Muslim parents in south west China. He grew up speaking both Arabic and Chinese which helped him in his later travels.

As a boy, he was captured by the Chinese army. He received an education and worked as a servant of a prince who later overthrew the emperor. Zheng served the prince well and helped him in wartime. The new emperor, Yongle, gave Zheng a fleet of ships and told him to sail to the countries beyond the horizon.

Over the years, Admiral Zheng sailed with about sixty-two ships to many lands, including present-day Vietnam, Indonesia, Malaysia, India, Somalia and Sri Lanka. He returned to China with jewels, ivory, exotic animals and spices.

Admiral
Zheng He

The Voyages of Admiral Zheng He

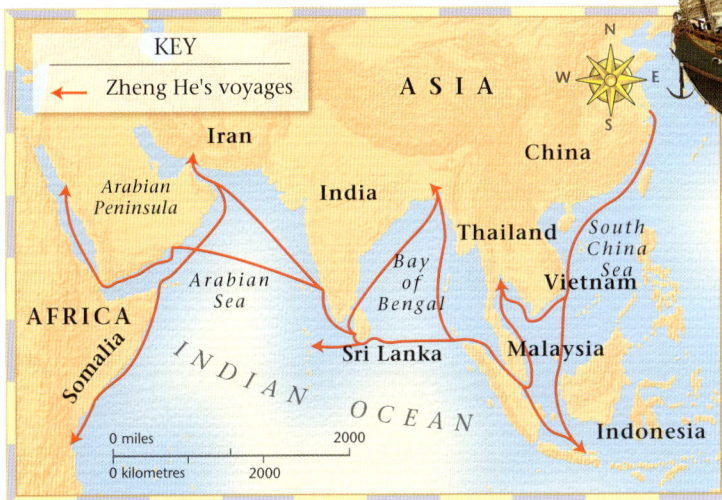

KEY

← Zheng He's voyages

ASIA

N
W E
S

Iran

China

Arabian
Peninsula

India

Thailand

South
China
Sea

Bay
of
Bengal

Vietnam

Arabian
Sea

AFRICA

Somalia

Sri Lanka

Malaysia

INDIAN OCEAN

Indonesia

0 miles   2000
0 kilometres   2000

Zheng He's fleet was made up of Chinese sailing vessels called junks.

7

Magellan Journeys West

Ferdinand Magellan

From 1519 to 1522 a European expedition led by Ferdinand Magellan became the first to sail around the globe.

In 1518 Magellan convinced King Charles I of Spain to pay for a voyage to the Spice Islands. These islands, now called the Moluccas, are part of present-day Indonesia. They were normally reached from Europe by sailing south past the west coast of Africa, then east into the Indian Ocean. Magellan believed the world was round. For this reason, he believed the trip would be shorter if he sailed west and went around the tip of South America. The expedition set out in 1519 with five ships and about 260 men. Magellan and his ships sailed through a dangerous passage and eventually reached the Pacific Ocean.

The Route of Magellan's *Vittoria*

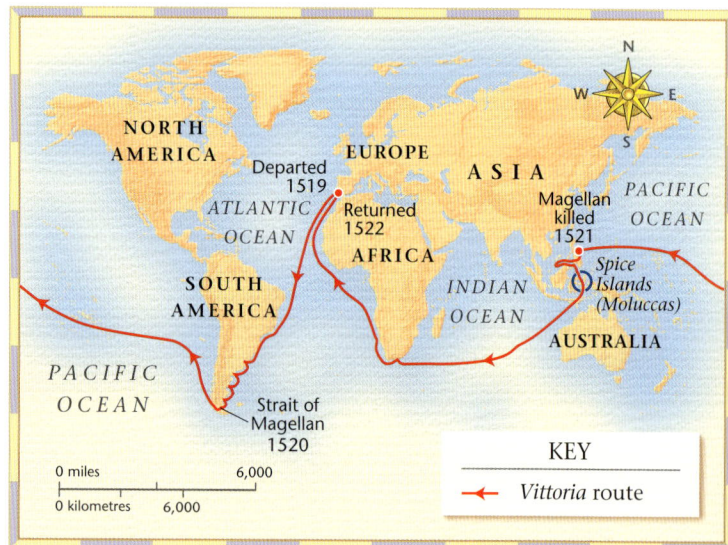

NORTH AMERICA

EUROPE

ASIA

Departed 1519

ATLANTIC OCEAN

Returned 1522

AFRICA

Magellan killed 1521

PACIFIC OCEAN

SOUTH AMERICA

INDIAN OCEAN

Spice Islands (Moluccas)

AUSTRALIA

PACIFIC OCEAN

Strait of Magellan 1520

0 miles   6,000

0 kilometres   6,000

KEY

Vittoria route

Two ships reached the Spice Islands, but only the *Vittoria* returned to Spain.

As early as 300 BC, the Spice Islands were visited often by Chinese, Indian and Arab traders in search of cloves and nutmeg.

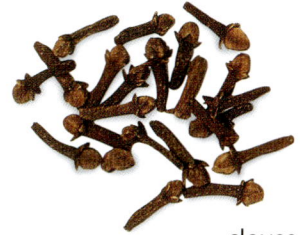

cloves

Magellan thought it would take about three weeks to reach the Spice Islands. Instead, it took about four months. Many of the sailors wanted to return to Spain, but Magellan pressed on. Eventually the food and water ran out. They had to eat bits of leather and sawdust. Nineteen men died before the fleet arrived in Guam and the sailors could restock their food and water. When the ships reached the Philippines, Magellan interfered in a war and was killed in battle.

nutmeg

Only two of Magellan's ships reached the Spice Islands, and only the *Vittoria* returned to Spain with a valuable cargo of spices. The crew of the *Vittoria* had sailed 81,450 kilometres, and became the first people to travel around the world.

Heyerdahl Crosses the Oceans

Thor Heyerdahl

Thor Heyerdahl (HI-ur-doll) believed that many ancient civilizations have had the same roots. He thought that the ancient Peruvians had travelled to islands in the Pacific on primitive boats. Maybe the ancient Egyptians had made similar voyages to America. To test his theories, Heyerdahl made several long and dangerous journeys.

In 1947 Heyerdahl built a raft with logs from the balsa tree. This is a light but very strong wood used by the ancient Peruvians. He called the raft the *Kon-Tiki*. Then he set sail from Callao in South America to Raroia Atoll, Polynesia, in the Pacific Ocean. It took him 107 days to travel 7,000 kilometres. He proved that South Americans could have migrated to Polynesia in ancient times and could have been the first settlers.

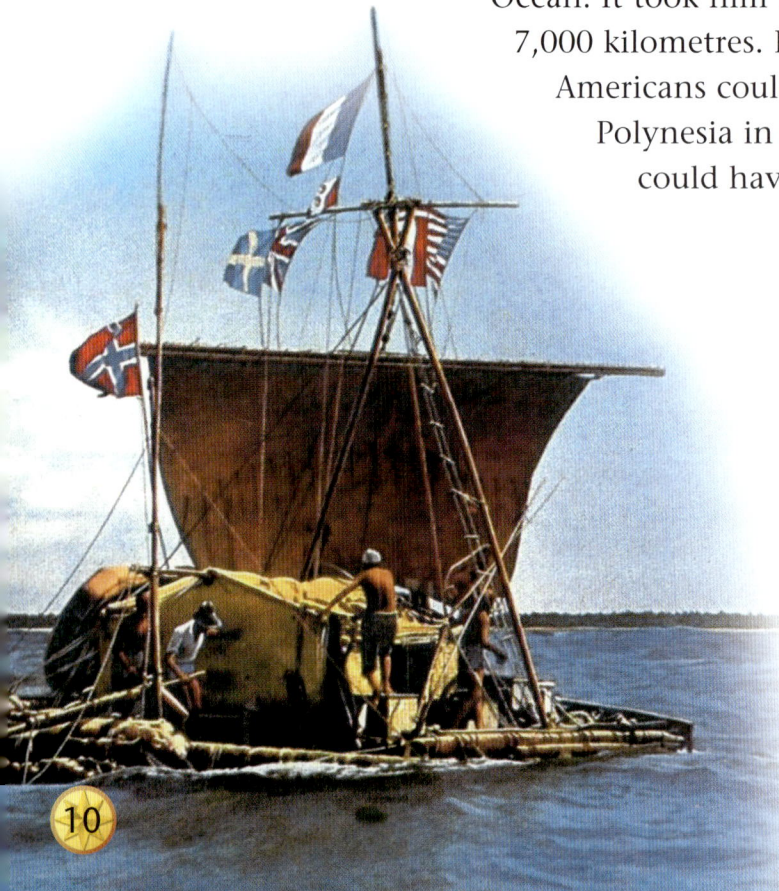

Heyerdahl sailed the *Kon-Tiki* from South America to Polynesia.

In 1969 Heyerdahl set sail in a reed boat called the *Ra* from Safi in North Africa to Barbados. He hoped to show that ancient Egyptians could have travelled the 5,262 kilometres in these simple boats. Just a week from Barbados, the *Ra* broke up and had to be abandoned. Heyerdahl then built a second boat based on the reed boats of Lake Titicaca. In 1970 he set sail again in his new boat called *Ra II*. This time, his journey was successful, proving that the ancient Egyptians could have reached the Americas.

Thor Heyerdahl sailed from North Africa to Barbados in the *Ra II*.

Thor Heyerdahl's Journeys

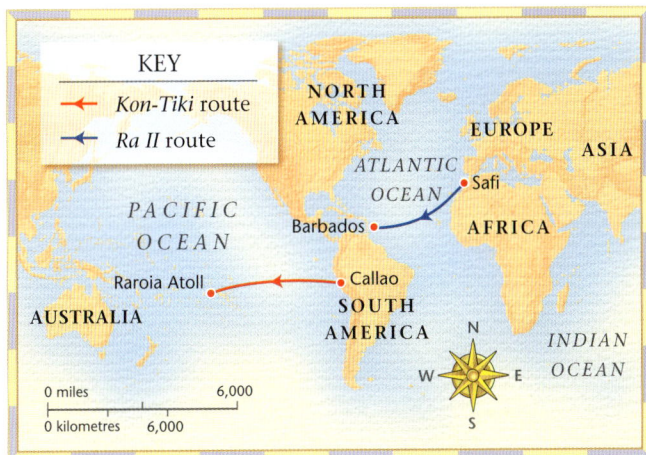

KEY

→ *Kon-Tiki* route
→ *Ra II* route

NORTH AMERICA
EUROPE
ASIA
ATLANTIC OCEAN
Safi
PACIFIC OCEAN
Barbados
AFRICA
Raroia Atoll
Callao
AUSTRALIA
SOUTH AMERICA
INDIAN OCEAN

0 miles   6,000
0 kilometres   6,000

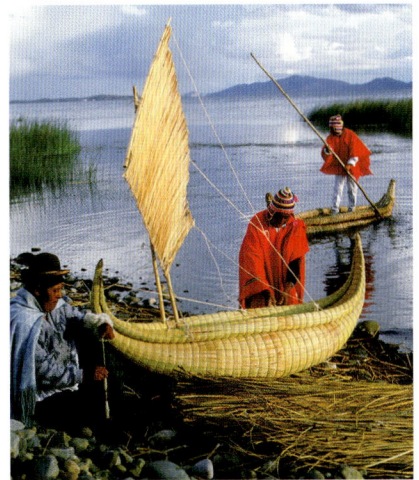

People who live near Lake Titicaca in South America still use boats made of reeds that grow beside the lake.

Train Travel

Most people today would not have wanted to travel on the first railways. The rails were made of wood or iron, and the trains were pulled by horses. The wooden seats were hard, and the ride was usually bumpy. These railways, however, were not meant for passengers. They usually carried coal. The first passenger coaches were used in 1825.

The Father of Railways

George Stephenson worked in a coal mine in the north of England. He ran and repaired the mine's steam-driven machinery. Stephenson built several locomotives for hauling coal, but not one that carried people. In 1825 he built the first train that carried people. He called it the *Locomotion*, and on 27th September 1825 he took it for its first ride. Cheered on by a crowd, the *Locomotion* travelled 13 kilometres and reached a top speed of 25 kilometres per hour.

George and Robert Stephenson were railway pioneers.

The *Locomotion* hauled a load of coal and flour and a special coach for passengers.

In 1829 the new Liverpool and Manchester Railway held a competition for the best railway engine. The railway was important because it would move cargo as well as transport people from Manchester factories to the port at Liverpool. Stephenson and his son Robert entered the competition with their engine called *Rocket*. Ten engines were entered for the competition, but only five engines arrived on the day of the competition. Two engines had mechanical problems so only three were working well enough to compete. Stephenson and his son won the prize of £500 when the *Rocket* reached a speed of 48 kilometres per hour.

a reproduction of Stephenson's *Rocket* locomotive

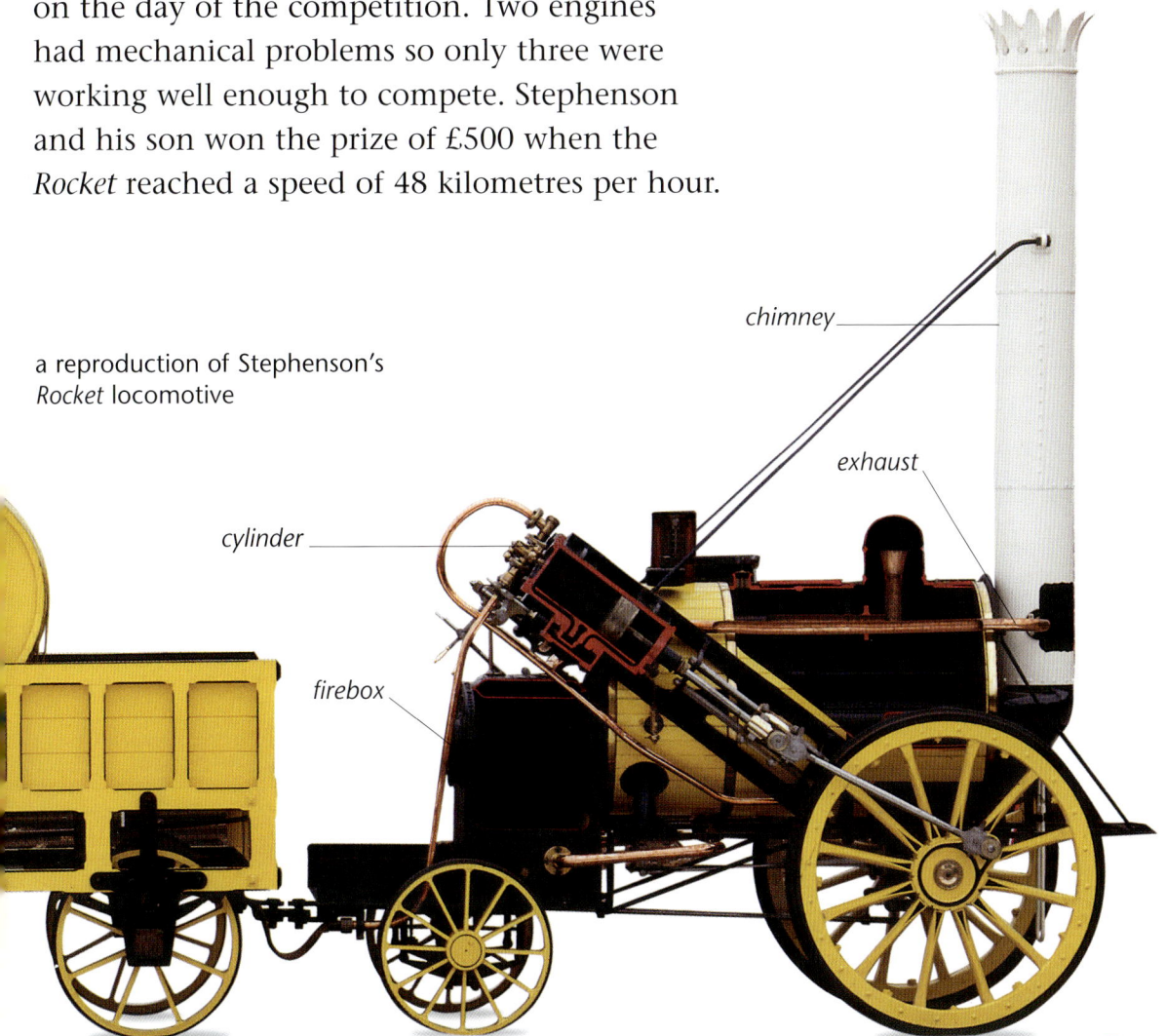

chimney

exhaust

cylinder

firebox

Uniting a Country by Rail

In 1871 British Columbia on the west coast of North America agreed to join Canada if the Canadian government promised to build a railway to connect it with the east of the country. So on 1st June 1875 work began.

Most of the railway was built between 1881 and 1885. It started in Montréal in the east and ended in Vancouver in the west. The tracks ran along sheer mountain sides, plunging deep into valleys and crossing wide rivers. A huge amount of dynamite was used to blast away rocks for the railway. Thousands of Chinese workers came to Canada to build the railway. Often they were given the most dangerous jobs, and many died. On 7th November 1885, the last spike was driven into the rail in Craigellachie, a town to the east of Vancouver.

The Canadian Pacific Railway engines travelled through forests, lakes and mountains.

Route of the Canadian Pacific Railway

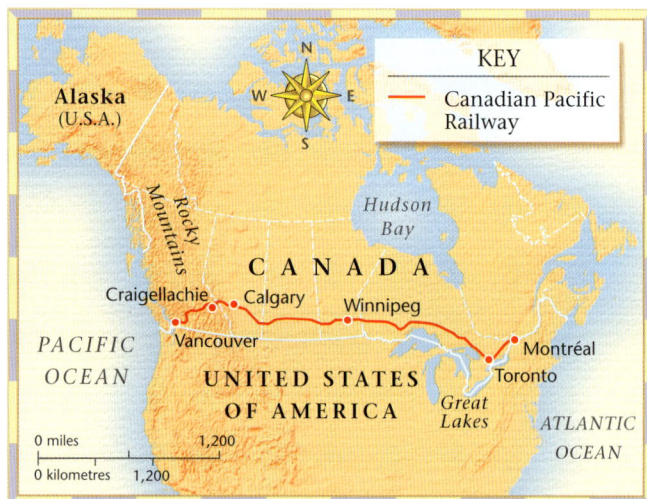

KEY
— Canadian Pacific Railway

Alaska (U.S.A.)

Rocky Mountains

Hudson Bay

CANADA

Craigellachie   Calgary   Winnipeg

PACIFIC OCEAN

Vancouver

Montréal

UNITED STATES OF AMERICA

Toronto

Great Lakes

ATLANTIC OCEAN

0 miles   1,200
0 kilometres   1,200

In 1886 Sir John A Macdonald, the prime minister, crossed the country on the railway with his wife, Lady Susan Agnes Macdonald. She wanted to sit at the front of the train – on the cowcatcher. Cowcatchers were designed to push wandering cows and other obstacles out of the train's way. Lady Macdonald rode on the cowcatcher for part of each day, seated on a wooden box tied to the front of the train. She enjoyed it so much that she announced, "I shall travel on this cowcatcher from summit to sea."

A Red Letter Day
For - Canada
June 28, '86
WHEN THE
CANADIAN PACIFIC
RAILWAY
OPENS PACIFIC
TO THE OCEAN

TRAIN LEAVES DAILY:
Toronto, - - 8.00 p.m.
Montreal, - - 8.00 "
Ottawa, - - 11.45 "

OUR OWN LINE
FROM THE
ATLANTIC TO THE PACIFIC
NO CUSTOMS   NO DELAYS   NO TRANSFERS
LOW RATES   QUICK TIME

railway poster

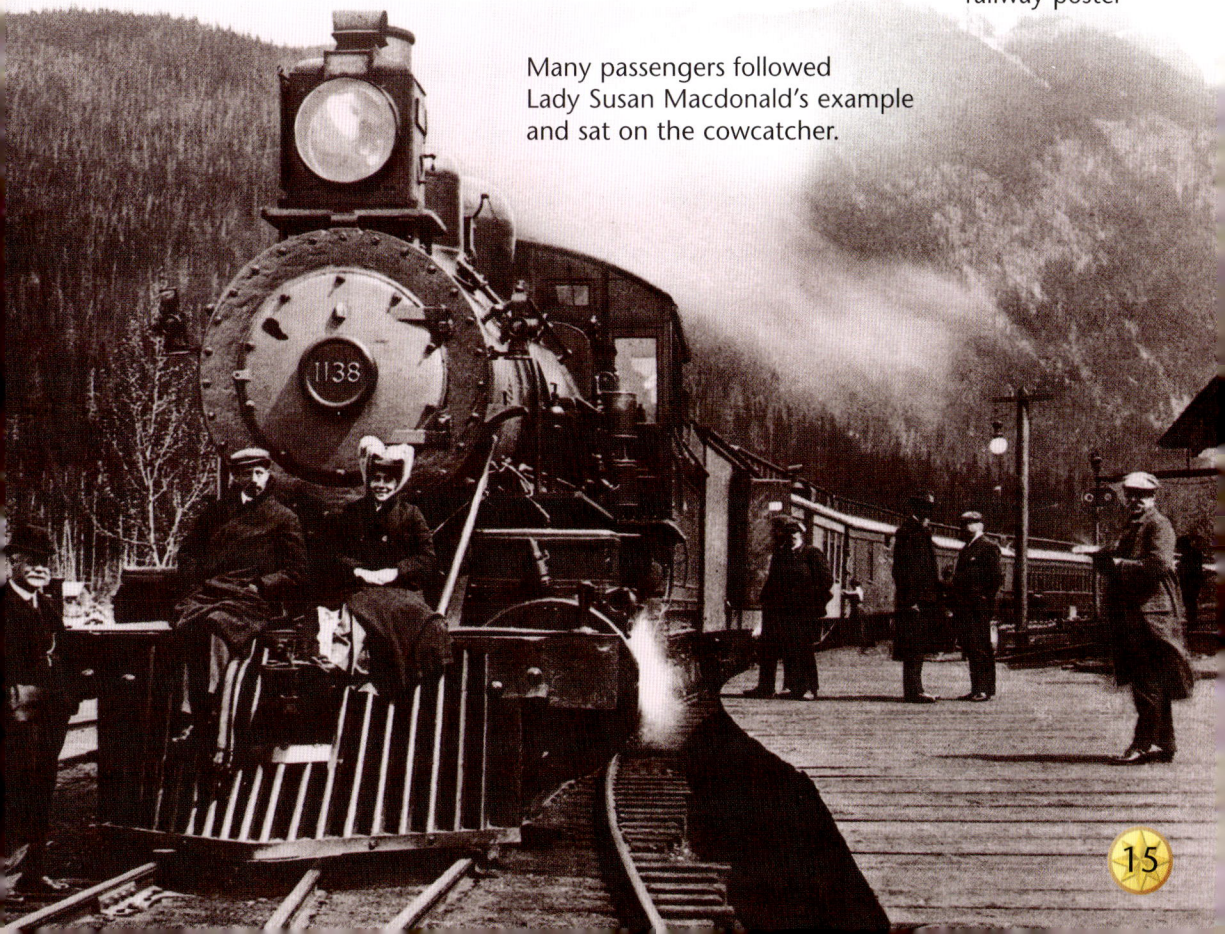

Many passengers followed Lady Susan Macdonald's example and sat on the cowcatcher.

Early Cars

Fifty years after steam-driven passenger trains began running, horse-drawn carriages were still used. Although trains were faster and more comfortable than the horse-drawn vehicles, many places could not be reached by trains.

Then "horseless carriages" were developed. Inventors of early cars tried many power sources. Some ran on steam, although other later cars used electricity. However, they were not very practical. A driver of a steam-powered car had to boil water to produce the steam to run the car. Drivers of electric cars couldn't go far without recharging the batteries.

Steam-powered "horseless carriages" didn't catch on as it was quicker to walk.

Karl Benz's Car

In 1885 a German inventor called Karl Benz designed and built the first car powered by petrol. It had three wheels, an electric battery, a spark plug and a water-cooled engine. It ran at top speeds of more than 8 kilometres per hour.

Benz kept working on his designs. Soon after 1890 he began selling a four-wheeled car called the Viktoria. It was followed in 1894 by another design called the Velo. So many people were interested in buying the Velo that Benz began thinking of ways to make more cars faster. In 1895 he produced sixty-two Velos – making the car the first produced in larger numbers.

Karl Benz

Benz's three-wheeler travelled at about the speed a person can run.

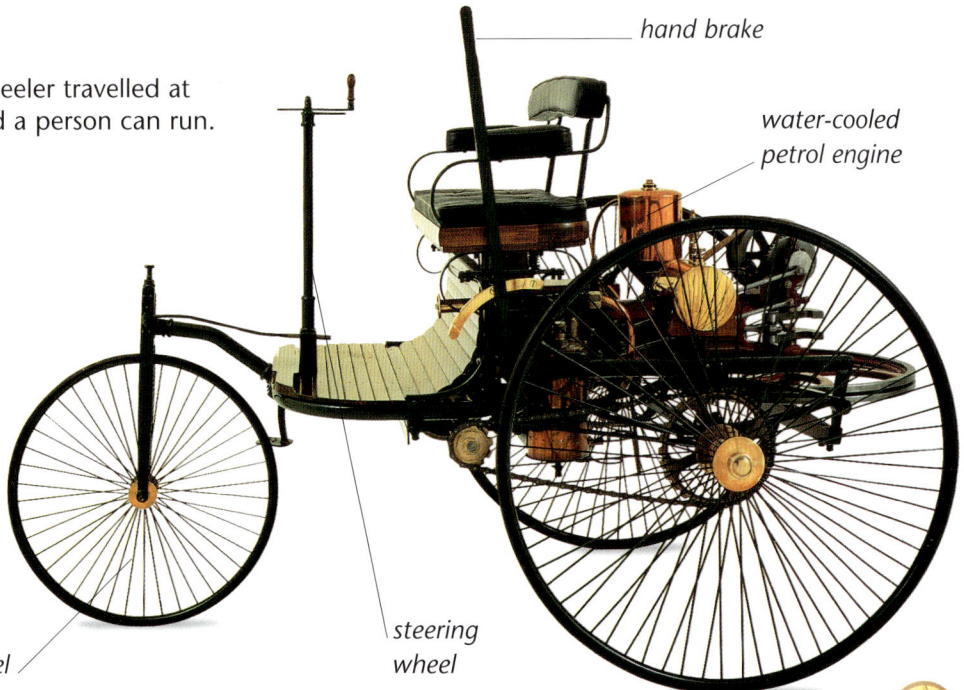

hand brake

water-cooled petrol engine

single front wheel

steering wheel

Henry Ford and the Model T

Henry Ford

In 1908 an American engineer called Henry Ford produced the first car that ordinary people could afford. His Model T car was easy to drive, reasonably priced and reliable. It became so popular that Ford had to find a new way to produce a huge number of cars.

Previously cars had been made by groups of two to three workers who built each car from start to finish. Ford started using the same parts, such as windows and headlamps, on all the cars. This cut time and costs, and greatly increased production. In 1913 Henry Ford set up assembly lines. Workers stood in one place and performed just one task on every car that moved past them. Ford also limited the choice of colours to save time. He said that people could have the Model T in "any colour, so long as it's black". When production of Model Ts ended in 1927, 15 million had been built.

Model T Ford

Ford's factory eventually cut production time for each car manufactured from days to minutes.

Driving Across Australia

In late 1907 Harry Dutton and Murray Aunger left Adelaide in a car called *Angelina*. They planned to cross Australia from south to north. They travelled across the dry centre of Australia, over sandy hills, stony plains and dry riverbeds. In many places there were no roads. Before they started their journey, camel trains dropped fuel and food at stops along the way.

Dutton and Aunger's Route

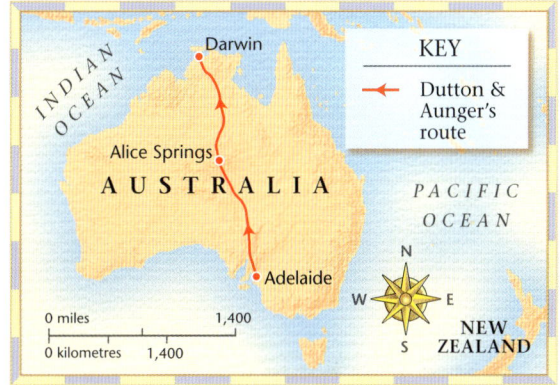

The south-to-north crossing lay over some of the most difficult landscape in Australia.

All went well until *Angelina* broke down. However, Dutton and Aunger went back to Adelaide and ordered a new, more powerful car. Several months later, the new car arrived from Britain. They set out again – this time, carrying spare parts. They found *Angelina*, repaired it and drove both cars side by side on to Darwin. On 20th August 1908 they completed the 3,200-kilometre journey in 51 days.

Dutton and Aunger crossed Australia from south to north in 1908 in this car.

First Flights

People have always dreamed of flying. Some built huge flapping wings and tried to fly like birds. Others built gliders: a type of aircraft without engines. Some travelled in hot-air balloons that drifted wherever the wind took them. Finally some people began to build aeroplanes.

The Wright Brothers' Flight

Flying fascinated Orville and Wilbur Wright. They were inventors who lived in Ohio in the United States. Orville and Wilbur made mechanical toys when they were boys. Later, they built and repaired bicycles. They wanted to be the first people to build and pilot a powered flying machine. They knew the first thing they needed was a lightweight engine.

Wilbur and Orville Wright

First they built a petrol engine with a propeller that was powerful enough to thrust, or push, an aircraft forwards. Next they built the body – with a compartment for the pilot to sit in. Then they built the wings so that air could flow over and under them. This would lift the plane into the air. At last the plane was ready. All they needed to do was test their invention.

Orville set up a camera to take this photograph before he took off.

Then on 17th December 1903 Wilbur and Orville set off with their plane to Kitty Hawk, North Carolina, USA. First the brothers tossed a coin to decide who would be the first to fly. When the wind was right, Orville took the controls.

He flew the plane down a hill where it wobbled uncertainly into the air. It remained airborne for about 35 metres, then landed safely on the ground. It had lasted for just 12 seconds, but it was a historic moment. It was the first time a pilot had flown an engine-powered machine.

The Wright brothers' propeller design was much more effective than other propellers of the time.

The Father of Aviation

In Brazil, Alberto Santos-Dumont is known as the Father of Aviation. Santos-Dumont built and experimented with hot-air balloons and gas-filled airships that could be steered.

In 1901 he won a prize of 100,000 francs for flying an airship around the Eiffel Tower. In 1904 he starting designing helicopters and gliders.

By 1906 Santos-Dumont had produced an extra-light flying machine that looked like three kites joined together. On 12th November 1906 Santos-Dumont flew his machine for 220 metres in a 21-second flight. It was the first powered flight made in Europe.

Santos-Dumont went on to design a flying machine called an ultra-light monoplane. This was a plane with only one set of wings. It weighed only 68 kilograms and was made of silk stretched over a bamboo frame. It was extremely popular, and Santos-Dumont sold thousands of copies. People called it the *Grasshopper* because of its insect-like appearance.

Alberto Santos-Dumont

Santos-Dumont crashed twice before completing the course that circled the Eiffel Tower.

First, Fastest and Best

Charles Lindbergh was the first person to fly solo non-stop across the Atlantic Ocean from New York to Paris. He took off from Long Island, New York, on 20th May 1927, in a single-engine monoplane, called the *Spirit of St Louis*. Thirty-three hours, 32 minutes and about 6,000 kilometres later, he landed safely in Paris.

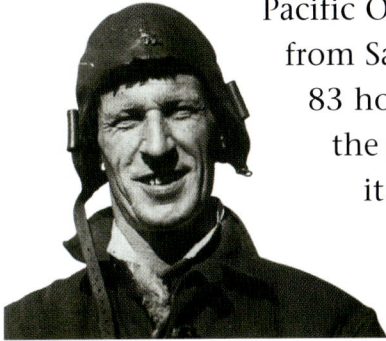

Charles Lindbergh's monoplane, the *Spirit of St Louis*

Charles Kingsford Smith was the first person to fly across the Pacific Ocean. His crew of four set off in 1928 from San Francisco, California, USA. It took 83 hours to travel 12,000 kilometres. When the plane reached Brisbane in Australia, it was met by 25,000 cheering people.

Charles Kingsford Smith

In 1930 Amy Johnson set out to fly from England to Australia. She faced bad weather, mechanical problems and crash landings. Johnson had to mend the canvas wings of her plane, *Jason*, along the way. It took her 19 days to travel 16,000 kilometres. Newspapers and radio reporters followed her adventures closely. When she landed in Darwin in Australia, Johnson was world-famous.

Amy Johnson

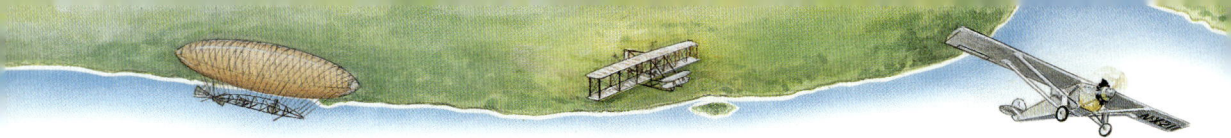

Amelia Earhart

Amelia Earhart

Amelia Earhart learned to fly soon after World War I. In 1928 she became the first woman to cross the Atlantic by air. She flew as a passenger, with two pilots called Wilmer Stultz and Louis Gordon.

After that, Amelia Earhart became very interested in long-distance flying, and she wanted to fly herself. In 1932 she became the first woman to fly solo across the Atlantic. Earhart set a new record for speed. It took her 13 hours and 30 minutes to fly from Newfoundland in Canada, to the British Isles.

Earhart began planning for a new goal. She wanted to fly around the world. After that, she planned to give up long-distance flying. In 1937, Earhart and her navigator, Fred Noonan, flew from California to Florida in a small two-engine plane. Noonan plotted a route from Miami that passed over Puerto Rico, South America, Africa, the Red Sea, India, Thailand, Singapore, Australia and landed in New Guinea. They took off on 1st June 1937 and reached New Guinea, on 29th June 1937. They had about 4,600 kilometres to go until their next stop at Howland Island in the north Pacific Ocean. From there they planned to return to the United States. They had enough fuel for about 20 or 21 hours of flight.

Somewhere over the ocean they lost radio contact. Despite an air and sea search no trace of the plane or its crew was found. In 2002 a marine biologist claimed to have seen a piece of the plane's wreckage on the small island of Nikumaroro. This claim is still being investigated, but so far Earhart's disappearance remains a mystery.

Amelia Earhart's Last Flight

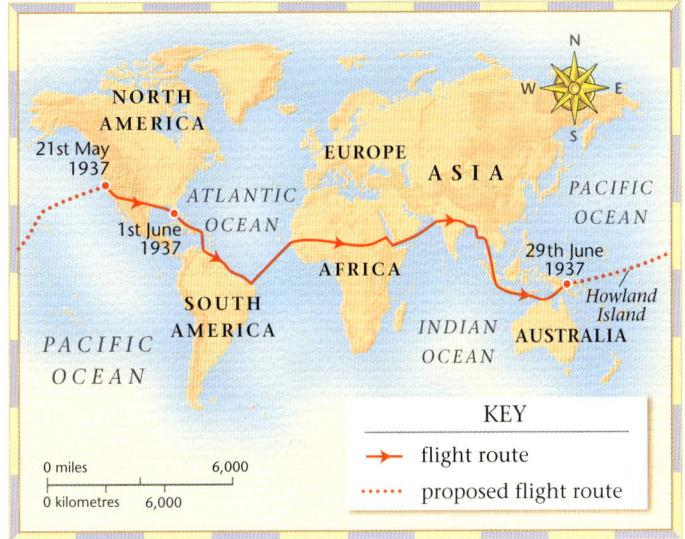

NORTH AMERICA

21st May 1937

EUROPE

ASIA

ATLANTIC OCEAN

1st June 1937

PACIFIC OCEAN

AFRICA

29th June 1937

SOUTH AMERICA

Howland Island

PACIFIC OCEAN

INDIAN OCEAN

AUSTRALIA

0 miles   6,000

0 kilometres   6,000

KEY

→ flight route

...... proposed flight route

Fred Noonan and Amelia Earhart looked over their plane before their flight.

Exploring Space

About fifty years after the first aeroplane flights, people began to think seriously about travelling into space. During the 1950s and 1960s the United States and Russia (then part of the Soviet Union) began a race to be the first to travel into space.

Sputnik I carried no living creatures on board.

First Satellites

In 1957 Russia successfully launched the first satellite, called *Sputnik I*. As it orbited, it sent back information about Earth's upper atmosphere. One month later, Russia launched *Sputnik II*. Scientists wanted to study the effects of space travel on a living animal, so this spacecraft carried a dog named Laika. Three dogs were trained to fly on a spacecraft. This would help scientists prepare to send people into space. Dogs were chosen because they are very similar to humans in the way they breathe and the way their blood flows. Laika did not live very long in space, but scientists learned from her experience and were able to improve conditions on the spacecraft.

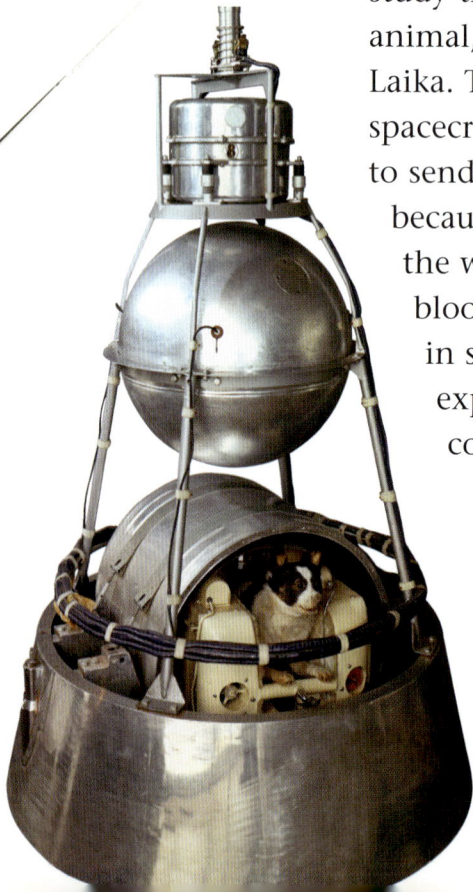

Laika in *Sputnik II*

First Human in Space

After Laika's flight, Russia sent several empty spacecraft into space to gather more data. Then on 12th April 1961 a Russian cosmonaut called Yuri Gagarin became the first person to orbit the Earth in *Vostok I*. He wore a specially designed spacesuit. It had multiple layers, a special breathing valve, a helmet and communications equipment. He travelled in a 2.5 metre capsule.

Yuri Gagarin

It took one huge rocket, plus four smaller booster rockets, to launch the capsule into space. The launch rockets were thirteen times bigger than Gagarin's tiny capsule. It took Gagarin 108 minutes to fly around the world once. Then he ejected from his spacecraft and parachuted safely to Earth.

Vostok 1 carried Gagarin into space.

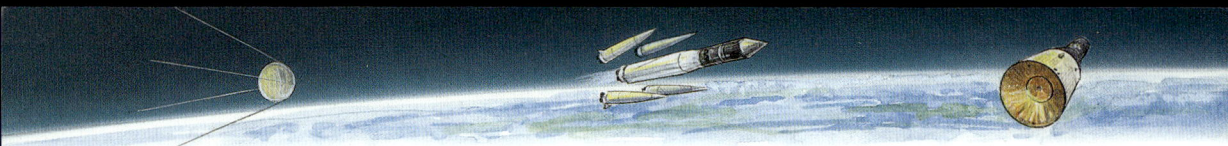

Man on the Moon

About a month after Gagarin's flight the first American astronaut Alan Shepard was launched into space. He made a successful 15-minute flight. President John F Kennedy then declared that an American would land on the Moon by the end of the 1960s.

During the 1960s Russia made some important achievements. In 1963 Valentina Tereshkova became the first woman in space. She spent nearly three days in orbit and circled the Earth forty-eight times. This was another victory for Russia. However, in 1966 Sergei Pavlovich died. He was the chief designer for the Russian space programme, so it was a terrible loss.

Meanwhile, the scientists at America's National Aeronautics and Space Administration (NASA) invented even more advanced spacecrafts.

Alan Shepard's rocket, *Freedom 7*, was launched in 1961.

Valentina Tereshkova

On 16th July 1969 *Apollo 11* took off from Florida with Neil Armstrong, Michael Collins and Edwin "Buzz" Aldrin. Its destination was the Moon. On 20th July 1969 millions of people all over the world crowded around televisions and radios as Neil Armstrong became the first man to walk on the Moon. His footprints are still visible there today.

Neil Armstrong, Michael Collins, and "Buzz" Aldrin

Then "Buzz" Aldrin joined Armstrong to become the second person to walk on the Moon. Michael Collins stayed in the orbiting command module. On the Moon, Armstrong and Aldrin planted an American flag. They collected rocks and soil samples and set up equipment that would continue to send information back to Earth after they had gone.

Aldrin joined Armstrong on the historic walk. They left footprints where none had been before.

The Space Shuttle

Over the next three years, several more American astronauts travelled to the Moon. In six separate *Apollo* flights, astronauts spent 80 hours walking on the Moon, taking photographs, collecting rocks, and setting up experiments. These space journeys were very expensive. A rocket used to launch the spacecraft could only be used once. So scientists worked on ways to make spacecrafts reusable.

On 12th April 1981 the first Space Transportation System, or space shuttle, orbited the Earth. Today a space shuttle can take astronauts and their equipment into space, then return to Earth to be used again. A space shuttle is huge and weighs more than 2,000 tonnes.

This space shuttle takes off from Florida.

A space shuttle is seen here with *Mir* space station.

flight deck

payload bay

vertical wing

A space shuttle can orbit Earth many times.

A space shuttle has three sections: an orbiter, a fuel tank and two rocket boosters. When a space shuttle is launched, two rocket boosters fall away after lift-off. They are recovered and reused while the fuel tank falls away and burns up after the shuttle reaches orbit. When the orbiter returns to Earth, it glides in and lands like a plane.

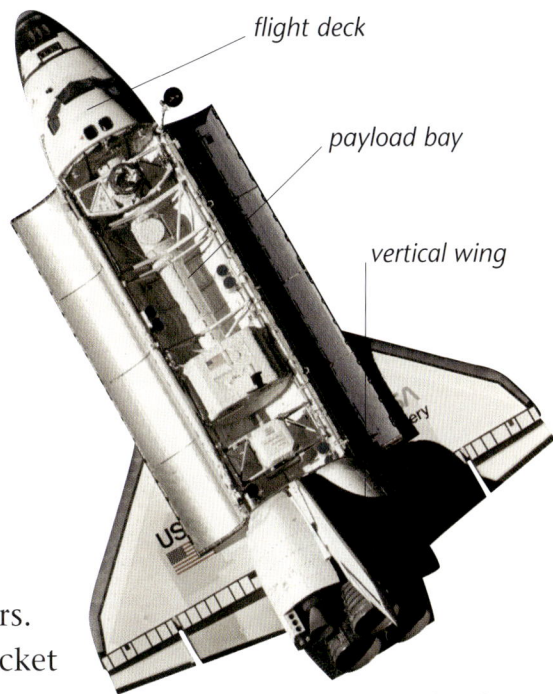

Where to Next?

So far we have only walked on the Moon. Now scientists are looking at our solar system's planets, wondering if humans could live on them. Where will humans journey to next? How will they get there? Who will be first? Like the adventurous men and women before them, people will continue to answer these questions as they journey into the universe's uncharted territory.

Index

562167